101 USES FOR AN EX-HUSBAND

by John C. Yurick and Marie Winslow

Illustrated by Kevin King

Published by Currier•Davis Publishing, Inc.

Cover design and book layout by
Kaye Michaels and Associates,
Longwood, Florida.

For information write:
Currier•Davis Publishing, Inc.
P.O. Box 58, Winter Park, Florida 32790-0058

ISBN: 0-930507-01-0
Library of Congress Catalog Number: 85-72280

**NOTE: Any resemblance, real or imagined, to actual people, living or dead, is purely
coincidental.**

Divorce — in and of itself — is not funny. Nor does it have to be tragic. After nearly 25 combined years in counseling and social work, the authors have watched this phenomenon spread throughout our society, changing the lives of many men, women and children.

Divorce is, nonetheless, a fact of life. And, as such, it is much more important for those whose lives it has touched to look for ways to make it bearable…if possible, to make it even laughable.

101 Uses For An Ex-Husband has been written to help you, the divorced woman, see that there *is* a silver lining to every dark cloud — even the one you've allowed your ex-husband to hang over your head.

This is not a "self-help" book; although the authors have suggested a number of ways in which you can use your ex-husband to help make your life easier.

It is not a joke book either; although humor has been used to highlight the bright side of your situation.

101 Uses For An Ex-Husband is subtle therapy…a book written to show you that you're not alone out there, that your life can be even better now that you have acquired a new tool for motivational growth: an ex-husband.

Read it and enjoy!

Table of Contents

Forward

Isn't life funny? Tragically funny! You spend half of it thinking about Mr. Right. Then one day, you think you've found him. As it works out, you marry him. Or he marries you. Years later, this is a moot point frequently brought up for torrid debate.

Then comes the tragic part. Mr. Right stops acting like Mr. Right. He starts acting like Mr. Dud, Mr. Macho, Mr. Ratfink, or two or three other Misters that come to mind. But *not* Mr. Right.

Now, somehow, you've managed to get to the point in your life where, among other things, you have acquired an *ex-husband.*

What the heck do you do with him?

Right now, the very idea of an ex-husband strikes fear in your heart. Let's face it — *it's a jungle out there!* You haven't played the dating game in quite a while and, boy, have the rules changed! Traps and pitfalls abound, and Lounge Lizards are just waiting to get their slimy claws on a sweet, inexperienced divorcee like you.

But hold on! An ex-husband can be a blessing in disguise. No longer do you have to dread dealing with him, thinking about him, or discussing him with others. You can actually start using him to your advantage! How?

101 Uses For An Ex-Husband will show you.

Throughout the ages, some of the wisest philosophers, poets, soothsayers, and grandparents have noted that there are at least two ways to look at every situation. ***101 Uses*** will show you a few more.

As you practice the techniques described herein, your confidence will grow. Your sense of humor will return. Life will be enjoyable again. You'll take that nasty jungle out there and turn it into your own personal playground. Just imagine: you, that once shy and scared little girl, becoming *Queen of the Jungle* — in charge of your life again!

Motivation with a capital "M" is the key. You may not have known it, but your ex-husband is a fantastic motivator. If he had motivated the people in his office as well as he now motivates you, he'd be another Lee Iacocca!

101 Uses will show you how to use your ex-husband as motivation for improving your mind, toning your body, strengthening your relationships, and stimulating your sex life! For despite what you may think, your "Ex" is not a useless albatross around your neck. There are, in fact, many advantageous uses for an ex-husband.

At *least* **101!**

CHAPTER 1

An ex-husband is great for your health.

I know that sounds absurd, especially after the fifty pounds you gained — or lost — during the separation and the divorce. And the number you did on your liver with all that booze. And the "medications" that put you in a near-comatose state trying to cope with him and the insanity of the situation. And now someone has the audacity to say that your ex-husband is good for your health?

It's true. An ex-husband is THE greatest asset to your physical well-being! And there are many ways you can use him to develop a healthy body. Not convinced? Read on.

1. **An ex-husband is useful for developing a running program.** How many times a day do you find yourself running back and forth to the mailbox, looking for alimony and child support checks that never seem to arrive? Forth and back, back and forth…through rain, snow, sleet, hail, and dead of night.

Haven't you ever wondered where the phrase "the check's in the mail" came from? Well, now you know. And the check will be there just infrequently enough to keep you at your running program day after day after day. You may die poor, but you'll die healthy!

2. **An ex-husband is useful for effective weight control and maintenance.** I know, thinking about "him" makes you so upset that you want to pig-out, but just remember some of the habits he exhibited during your marriage: the belching, the knuckle cracking, the snoring. A jumbo jet landing in your driveway would have been quieter! Remember the way he always left the toilet seat up and *still* missed the target! Or how about those smelly cigars, and his weekend habit of not shaving or showering…even after mowing the lawn or working on that greasy car! And don't forget his late-night partying and the way he started showering and shaving for "her."

How do those thoughts help with weight control? They're enough to make you sick! And it's difficult to put on weight that way!

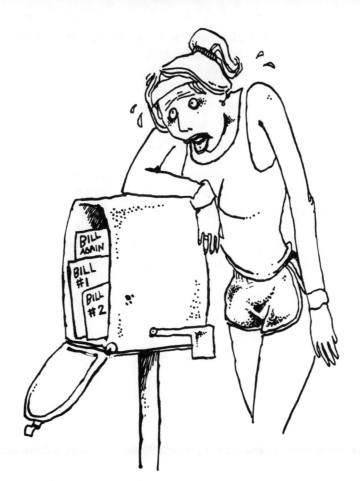

3. **An ex-husband is excellent motivation for joining health clubs, health spas and exercise classes.** You've seen some of those sweet young bimbos he's been dating since the divorce and you'll be damned if that nineteen-year-old's figure will be better than yours! It's unfortunate that you didn't see some of his really gross dates. But if you had you wouldn't be so motivated to shape up now. Besides, wouldn't it be nice to show him exactly what he's given up?

An ex-husband is also excellent motivation for getting specific body parts in shape:

4. **Breast Augmentation.** If it weren't for the divorce, you probably wouldn't have had the boob-job. Now that he's not around, it's important to feel good about yourself again. Not to mention looking stunning in your new "non-swimming" bathing suit.

Having children certainly did little, if anything, to promote your shape. And Ratfink sure didn't help. Now, with the "support" of that handsome surgeon, and the motivation of your "Ex," you've managed to put new meaning into the question: "Have you seen your feet lately?"

5. **Upper-Body Strength.** Dart-throwing comes immediately to mind. Not only will it improve your hand-eye coordination, it might just give you the best biceps around! For practice, use that bountiful supply of his pictures you have lying around. Especially the ones you found of him and "her."

You might also get a measure of personal satisfaction from seeing a dart hanging out of Ratfink's ear...or some other part of his anatomy.

6. **Cardiovascular System.** Use your ex-husband to strengthen your heart. Think of the jolts it received every time he did something unexpected. Like when you discovered he had cleaned out the joint bank account to go yachting with that bevy of busty blondes? Or when you found out he was "dating" (HA!) your best friend? How about all the exercise your heart got — and maybe still gets — when you worried about him, feared for him, or got angry with him? When you really stop to think about it, he's better for your cardiovascular system than the Jane Fonda Workout!

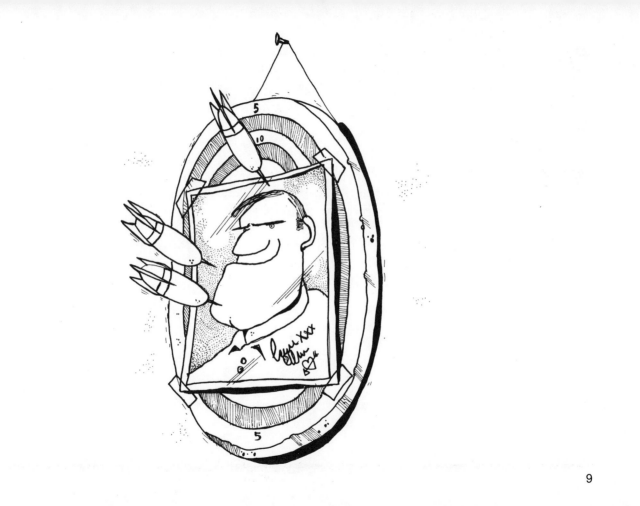

7. Migraine Relief. Having an ex-husband can actually help rid you of these nasty headaches. Remember how he said you had them every time he wanted to "make love" (or, as you called it, "put-up-with-his-sexual-moans-and-grunts")? And he always complained that you were such a headache to him. Come to think of it, headaches were one of the few things you two had in common towards the end.

But now that he's gone, so are your migraines. Hopefully, he still has his.

8. Facial Aerobics. If your ex-husband is living within a few thousand miles of you, the teeth-clenching and grimacing comes automatically. These exercises ensure that a face-lift will never be necessary. And there is no chance that you will ever develop a double-chin.

9. Dental Hygiene. With all that clenching and gnashing of teeth, it's time for you to visit the dentist for some attractive caps. While there, ask that cute dentist for his advice about the sexiest brand of toothpaste. And be sure to have the bill sent to Ratfink.

CHAPTER 2

Financial Management

An ex-husband can be used to help you understand the basics of financial management ...no matter who came out ahead in the divorce settlement.

The terms "deficit spending," "extension of money," and "extension of ground beef" are becoming painfully clear. However, you can use your ex-husband — and the little things he left behind — to save money for yourself.

This is just as important if you were the financial "winner." (Besides, divorce attorneys are the only really *big* winners.) And despite all the whining your "Ex" does about how you took him to the cleaners, we all know that he *did* manage to hide some valuable assets.

Now's your chance. Don't get mad...get even!

10.

Use the things your ex-husband left behind as a tax deduction for yourself. All you have to do is get them together and call the Salvation Army. Sure, he took all the good stuff, but there's a closet full of leisure suits and polyester pants that he swore would come back into style. Perhaps you can strike a bargain with a charitable group to spread rumors that your ex-husband's suits are showing up all over Skid Row!

One caution: he might have left those things behind intentionally. It provides him with an excuse to check up on you. A safety net in case he has second thoughts about the divorce. You don't really think he's calling at 2:00 a.m. because he wants his Nehru jacket back, do you?

You may even be tempted to use these things as an excuse to check up on him. But who'd believe you stopped by at 6:00 a.m. Sunday morning to return a left-handed monkey wrench he never used?

Avoid that temptation.

11. **Use your ex-husband's things to barter for services.** Offer to let the neighborhood kids use his old clothes for Halloween costumes in exchange for lawn work. Trade his new tennis racquet for private dance lessons from that cute bachelor down the street. Swap his old tools for auto repairs from the handsome mechanic at the corner station. Isn't this fun?!

12. **Use his *really* old clothes for your vegetable garden.** Make a scarecrow out of the things the kids didn't even want. The birds will be too frightened to ever bother your tomatoes again, and your garden will become the envy of your friends. You might even win the "Best Scarecrow" award from the local garden club.

13. **Use your ex-husband's "toys" in more practical ways.** You can use his old bowling ball as an anchor for your new boat. It'll save you some money and make an excellent conversation piece.

14. **Use your ex-husband's things to save on winter heating costs.** Save yourself the hassle and expense of buying kindling for the fireplace. Just use his favorite chair and all those unfinished projects in his workroom. Won't it be fun to find out what the melting point of a golf club is?

15. **Use the things he left behind to make extra money.** You can use all his old love letters — including the ones you found to "her" — to write plots for daytime soap operas. Of course, nobody will believe them. The stuff they contain is even too bizarre for "Dynasty"!

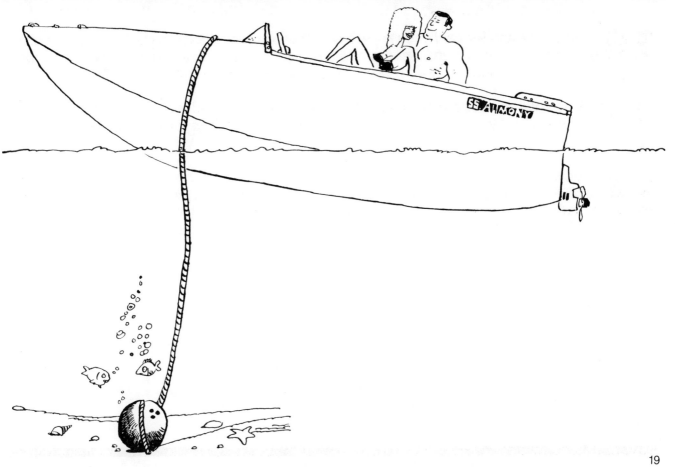

16. **Sell his trash for cash.** You know that collection of so-called "classic literature" he kept? Right...the porno mags. Sell them as a pilot for X-rated cable programs. No, on second thought, don't sell them. You might want to keep them for your own bachelorette parties.

17. **Use your ex-husband to avoid donation-seekers.** Instead of telling them that you "gave at the office," you can say that your office will be happy to give for you...then give them his address.

18. **Use your ex-husband to expand your credit line.** Your ex-husband makes an excellent source of credit for opening new charge accounts at really expensive stores. He probably won't agree to this immediately, so be prepared for a trade-off. Tell him you won't open an account with the local escort service if he agrees to the expensive clothing stores. That should persuade him.

CHAPTER 3

An ex-husband, and the entire divorce experience, can be used to help you pursue a variety of exciting careers.

Perhaps you think it's difficult to start a new career. Not with your "Ex"-perience, it's not! Thanks to your ex-husband, you already have an impressive resume of practical, on-the-job training in law, finance, psychology and detective work. You've even become something of a music critic. Not convinced? Check it out.

19. **Use your "ex" to become a wealthy financier.** Marriage is actually a lot like money. You see, "love" grows in direct proportion to the amount of "interest" paid, and if the interest is too low, then it's just not worth the "investment." But you know that already. Apply this rule to your financial investments and watch the money roll in. Thanks, "Ex"!

20. **Use your "ex" to become a philosopher.** After all, your ex-husband did give you a new outlook on those old marriage vows. Marrying "for richer or poorer" was one thing, but you've discovered that it's much better to "divorce for richer." There must be a career choice in there somewhere!

21. **Use your "ex" to become a private eye.** Remember how you uncovered the truth about Ratfink's philandering? Remember how skillfully you tracked down all of his hidden assets during the divorce? Haven't you noticed yourself talking more and more like a female Mike Hammer? Now you can use your investigative skills to help other women facing the same challenge. Hey…Sherlock Holmes had nothing on you!

22. **Use your "ex" to start a career in psychology.** Your ex-husband helped you develop a Freud-like skill for spotting rationalizations and defense mechanisms. Remember how you listened to his ludicrous explanations when you caught him lying, cheating and wenching? Remember how you kept analyzing him, the situation, and especially yourself? Remember how nutty your early conclusions were?

See how much saner your conclusions have become? See how much sound psychological advice you're now able to offer friends? Notice how they don't take your advice either? Someday they'll wish they'd listened!

23. **Use your "ex" to begin a career in law.** During litigation over custody and property settlements, your ex-husband was useful in helping you learn the strategies that all great lawyers know: find your opponent's weakness and then you (and your mean, greedy and unscrupulous divorce attorney) go for it!

Remember all those harried phone calls and meetings with your attorney? It seemed as if the whole world was at stake! And how about all those sessions with your friends — the amateur "para-legal people" — over coffee? After all you've been through, you're almost ready to hang out your own shingle!

27

24. Use your "ex" to enhance your music appreciation. Because of Ratfink, the words to these old songs now have more meaning:

- **"Your Cheatin' Heart"**...the way you felt when you first discovered his infidelities.
- **"Poor Side of Town"**...the song your ex-husband is singing since you and your attorney took him to the cleaners.
- **"Killing Me Softly"**...the way you used to feel when he put you down, criticized you, or compared you unfavorably (was there any other way?) with others.

Let's face it. You now listen to the radio with an entirely new perspective. Think of how often you yell "HAH!" to mushy love songs with their promises of lifelong affection. In fact, you've revamped your list of personal "favorites" completely:

- **"Beat It"**...sung with a gusto that makes Michael Jackson look sick.
- **"What's Love Got To Do With It?"**...notice how often you ask yourself the same question?
- **"Strut, Pout!"**..."Watch me baby while I walk out that door..."echoes in your soul as some "lounge lizard" tells YOU how much you need HIM!!

Now that's music appreciation!

29

25. **Use your "ex" to become a famous writer.** Just think of all those "nasty-grams" and hate letters you've written. You know, the ones you never sent. How about those romantic novels you constantly fantasize? Or the "short stories" about "Sex Life With Ratfink"? Don't let this skill go to waste. Submit some articles to **Penthouse, Playboy** and **Hustler.** Use his real name.

26. **Use your "ex" to increase your vocabulary.** Look at the ways Ratfink has helped you expand your reading. From legal paperwork to "how-to" books and personal advice columns. What about the new language you've learned from your shrink? And then there are all those foul phrases you find yourself muttering when Ratfink comes to mind. With this increased vocabulary, you're either ready to become a librarian or a truck driver.

CHAPTER 4

Divorce or no divorce, if there are children involved, you will be seeing your ex-husband. And seeing him when he comes over to pick up the kids will probably cause you to experience a myriad of feelings.

You might feel **Sadness,** and start asking yourself if the divorce was really necessary. Of course, if you think about it for a milli-second you know the answer is a resounding **YES!**

You might feel **Guilt** — especially when reviewing the fun you had with your new boyfriend the night before, while your ex-husband was baby-sitting the kids. Just remind yourself of all those lonely nights *you* spent with the kids while he was out with his harem before the divorce! That should earn you some guilt-fighting points!

You might feel **Regret.** Hopefully, it will be regret that it took you so long to wise up and file for divorce!

You might even feel **Rage** when he comes to pick up the kids. Instead of waiting for the kids in the car, as any well-trained ex-husband should, Ratfink comes inside, raids your refrigerator, and plops down in his favorite chair. After all he's done to you, that takes a lot of nerve!

You might even feel **Sorry** for him. He looks so tired, broke and burned-out. It may really bother you to see him looking so down.

Well, you'd better wake up to the *real* reason he looks this way. He know's it's a great way to manipulate you. He's looking for a little pity, not to mention a meal and a shoulder to cry on.

The **Truth** of the matter is this: he deliberately wears his oldest, shabbiest clothes so you'll think he's broke. He doesn't want you to know how many millions he has stashed away. If you found out about his fancy new sports car — the one he bought to go with his "new image" — you and your greedy divorce attorney would probably sue him for an increased settlement. And the real reason he looks so tired is that he's trying desperately to keep pace with his new teen-queen!

But don't despair. Start using your ex-husband's visitation privileges to your own advantage.

27. **Use your ex-husband as a garbage disposal.** You know how hard it is to clean out the refrigerator. Why bother? Let Ratfink do it for you. Put the month-old leftovers up front. He's bound to eat them. Just be sure to hide the Beef Wellington, Asparagus Souffle, and Chocolate Mousse you've prepared for your new boyfriend. Otherwise, Ratfink will eat them, too!

28. **Use your ex-husband as an auto service.** He's perfect for flat tires and minor mechanical repairs. After all, you need the car to shop for "his" kids or they'll starve. (This is one of those times when your kids are referred to as "his kids.") This tactic also works when the kids need a chauffer and you need a break. At first, just pretend the car is broken. Fixing an "un-broken" car is good for his ego and probably within his limits. Besides, it gives him the confidence to tackle the job when it's *really* important.

37

29. **Use your ex-husband as a maid service.** Appeal to his sympathy. Tell him you're exhausted from trying to be both father and mother to "his" kids, and you just don't have the energy to vacuum, mop and dust. Tell him the Health Department is threatening to condemn your home, which would reflect poorly on his community image and force the kids to come live with him! If you get especially good at pushing his guilt buttons, you might even have him doing windows!

30. **Use your ex-husband as a gardener.** Remind him that the job of mowing, raking and edging the lawn is just too hard for you to handle. Tell him that good help is expensive and, as it is, you're barely getting by on his current alimony payments. Tell him you'd really *hate* to see them increase.

31. **Use your ex-husband as an errand boy.** Whatever you need — prescriptions, pizza, pantyhose — get him to pick it up on his way to the house. Tell him you're too busy with "his" kids and just can't get away. Using Ratfink as an errand boy saves you a lot of gas, not to mention the inconvenience and hassle of rush-hour traffic. In fact, your ex-husband can be an excellent home-delivery service for businesses that didn't even know they delivered!

32.

Use your ex-husband as a handyman. Start out by asking him to fix the kids' broken bicycles and doll carriages. While he's at it, get him to replace storm windows, paint walls, walk the dog and dispose of the garbage. Of course he didn't do those things when he lived there, but on some level, even a schmuck like him is probably feeling a little guilty. If he isn't feeling guilty enough, tell him that you've been dating a pilot. He flies locally. He's a skywriter.

Initially he's going to balk at some of these suggestions. To motivate him, casually mention that your attorney thinks it's time to take him back to court for more money. And that you have an excellent chance of winning.

If that doesn't work, subtly hint that you and the kids are thinking about moving to another country. Leave brochures of Italy, France and Spain lying around the house.

Or tell him that you've been planning to take in a boarder or two…or twenty. Explain that this would increase your money supply and give you some help around the house. Mention that the Hell's Angels are looking for a new club house. Even Ratfink has a breaking point!

Once you have located his motivation button, use Ratfink as a jack-of-all-trades and stash away the money you're saving. Put it towards a new mink or a Caribbean cruise. Best of all, you'll have finally found a way to make his visitations bearable!

41

CHAPTER 5

An ex-husband is used for a dynamite sex life. You're probably wondering how that's possible. After all, you were married to him for what seemed like an eternity... and you're a little gunshy after the twin agonies of separation and divorce. It never occured to you that Ratfink could actually be useful when you re-enter the dating game. In fact, the idea of singles bars and lecherous men-on-the-make might scare the hell out of you! But eventually, you're going to get bored sitting at home, dwelling on the past, playing the old songs, and whining about how lousy your ex-husband turned out to be.

So instead of waiting for the next "Mr. Right" to find you, you're going to get bored enough— sometimes even horny enough — to go out and start looking for him. And whether you look in singles' bars, the country club or the laundromat, you're eventually going to meet someone.

At that point, you can use your ex-husband to help your sex life become something that XXX-rated movies would envy! How? Wouldn't *you* like to know?

33. **Use your ex-husband as a babysitter.** While the kids are spending weekends and holidays with Ratfink, you and your new boyfriend are free to explore the delights of "motion lotion," body painting, and all those Oriental positions you've heard so much about. Who knows, you might actually discover that you do have a G-Spot! Just be sure to stay in shape. Otherwise, you'll end up flat on your back in the chiropractor's office.

34. **Use your ex-husband as an excuse for any initial shyness.** You might be a little scared when your new lover suggests things that your mother told you "good girls shouldn't do." Explain that your ex-husband was so sexually inept that you just never imagined that there were so many exciting ways to make love. Tell him you're really not inhibited, just "demurely uneducated," and willing to learn!

35. **An ex-husband is used to turn your new lover into a "Marathon Man"!** Just tell him that your ex-husband was sexually motivated only once or twice a month. And that love-making lasted about 10 minutes if the television was on — five if it was off. Mention that you've heard stories about people who do it twice in the same night, but three times is unbelievable! Especially if you were to have an orgasm each time! If that doesn't motivate him, check his pulse!

36. **Use your ex-husband to improve your lover's technique and creativity.** All you need to do is tell your new lover that the only position your "Ex" knew was the missionary one. Tell him how boring Ratfink was in bed, and about how the closest he ever brought you to the "Big O" was the balance in your checkbook. Present this information as a challenge. Your new lover will be constantly motivated to bring you to new erotic heights. No red-blooded male would ever want you to think he's as bad in bed as your "Ex"!

37. **Use your ex-husband as a sexual yardstick.** See how your new lover measures up to Ratfink when it comes to positions, intensity, frequency, and duration. It's bound to be an improvement! Do enough of these "comparisons" (call it "research" if you like), and you might replace Dr. Ruth or Masters & Johnson as the world's greatest "sex-pert"!

38. **Use your ex-husband as a date source.** Now you can openly do what his best friends secretly suggested throughout your marriage. Call Ratfink for their phone numbers. Ask him about their status. Question him about the new hunk who started working in his office just before you separated.

39. **Use your ex-husband as an easy bedmate.** Why not? Sometimes, it's actually useful to be with your ex-husband. It gives you a new perspective. After all, "great" has a lot more meaning when you have an "awful" with which to compare it.

If you have any qualms about bedding down with Ratfink, just think of it as charity work. Let him wonder where you learned all those new moves. Besides, it's good reinforcement if you ever start wondering why you divorced him in the first place.

CHAPTER 6

Relationships

An ex-husband can be useful in establishing better relationships with your parents, your former in-laws, and your friends. You probably thought divorce had destroyed family life and friendships as you knew them. Your mother-in-law is now convinced that you're the gold digger and shrew she always suspected. Your friends have taken sides in the divorce and some have stopped talking to you. Good riddance to those turkeys! Hell, it was embarrassing enough to know that they were aware of his philandering long before you even suspected!

The kids are confused about who caused the divorce. And the thought of either of you remarrying is out of the question. In fact, they'll go to great lengths to sabotage any "serious" relationships either of you develop. Unless your new boyfriend is head of Disneyland, Mattel Toys, or Hershey's Chocolate, you're in for big trouble. They only tolerate Ratfink's girlfriend as long as she takes them to pizza parlors, video arcades or McDonalds, and never says "no" to anything they want. Come to think of it, that's why Ratfink likes her, too.

It's time for you to stop feeling badly about changed and complicated relationships. If you play your cards right, you can use the divorce as a way of decreasing hassles for yourself and improving the overall quality of your relationships.

40. **An ex-husband is used to keep your father in good physical shape.** Everytime your "Ex" neglects the children or does something bizarre to you, tell your father. You know how your father likes to share in your misery, and how he always overreacts. These jolts will help to strengthen his cardiovascular system. Just use good judgment in revealing the latest shocks, and you'll have given your father an excellent heart conditioning program.

41. **Your ex-husband is used to increase your father's golf skills.** Every time your father is on the golf course, he can think about all the money he loaned your ex-husband, and how he never received a dime in return. This is guaranteed to make him so angry that he will pretend the golf ball is Ratfink, resulting in longer drives and fewer mishit balls. It will also help to lower your father's golf score, leading to a four handicap and clubhouse bragging rights.

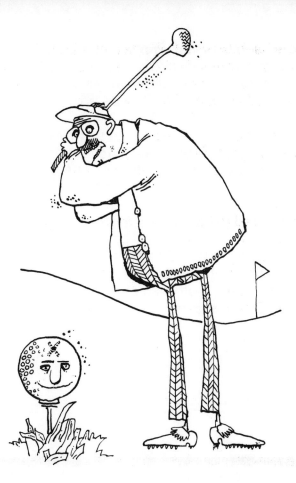

42. **An ex-husband is used to boost your father's ego.** At cocktail parties, your father can swap horror stories with his friends about the disgusting, low-down things your ex-husband has done. It's sure to make him the center of attention. After all, the things Ratfink does are more outrageous than anything on "Dallas." In no time, he'll be able to walk into any room and command immediate attention.

This confidence will carry over into his business decisions, his investment strategies, and even his sex life. Of course, your mother will get mad at you because she thought all that sexual nonsense was over with. Placate her by pointing out that dad's confidence has increased his earnings, thus allowing them to take separate vacations.

43. **An ex-husband is used to boost your mother's ego, too.** Remember: mothers relish war stories even more than fathers. Dad gets caught up in the moral rights and wrongs of the situation. Mom adds the "gossip factor." She can even change the name if the story is a little too personal. This means added prestige at bingo, coffee klatches, and bridge parties.

Again, this confidence will carry over into other areas. None of which will please your father...except maybe the separate vacations. Otherwise, she'll drive him nuts rehashing your latest tragedy.

55

44. **An ex-husband is used to get sympathy from your mother.** All you have to do is tell Mom that Ratfink never did like her. "Remember how he always wanted to go to his parents' house for the holidays? That's because he never could stand you, Mother." Tell Mom he always thought she was overweight. And a lush. And that her clothes always looked like they came from a second-hand store. And that he never liked any of her gifts. Make this stuff up if you have to. Once she hears what a fiend you put up with, the sympathy will flow.

45. **An ex-husband is also used to get your mother's approval.** You know what that is. You always wanted it. Someone else always got it. No matter how good your grades were …no matter how many chores you did around the house, some slob sister, brother, cousin, or neighbor always got your mother's approval. Well, thanks to your ex-husband, your time has finally come.

Just remind Mom of Ratfink's favorite phrase: "like mother, like daughter." Tell her that he kept seeing more and more of her in you. In fact, one of the reasons he left was because he dreaded to think that you might someday look, act, and nag the way your mother does.

Pretty soon, Mom will be on your side. She'll begin to point out that you *do* have some of her traits. Bite your tongue and agree. This is the approval you've always wanted.

46. **An ex-husband is used to improve relationships with your in-laws.** You now have an excuse for seeing them as little as possible. You no longer have to put up with boring family reunions, monotonous vacations, or repetitive stories about their son's childhood sweetheart and "what a wonderful daughter-in-law she would have made." And with Ratfink gone, they'll visit you less often, thus reducing those dreadful "white glove" inspections. Where do you think the term "Snoopy Sniffer" came from anyway?

47. **An ex-husband is used to establish honest communications in a family.** Now that you're divorced, your family never has to see him again. And all your relatives will be happy to tell you they didn't like him — even before the marriage. Some relatives *do* sound a little "I-told-you-so-ish," but that's to be expected. Especially relatives who pull you aside and want advice on how they can get the same results. Mass hysteria could result.

48.

An ex-husband can be used to form friendships with other women. It has been said that a dog is man's best friend. Fortunately, a woman can be another woman's best friend. And Ratfink can be instrumental in strengthening this bond.

Many of your friends have their own ex-husbands, and can really understand what you're going through. Just don't be too successful in handling Ratfink. If your friends start to feel inferior, they'll look for another support person. One as miserably human as they are.

Some married women will avoid you once you're divorced. They'll see you as a threat. Imagine that!! You! A threat?! Why, just a few months ago, you felt totally unlovable. Now these women have you pegged as some wanton beauty poised to steal their man. Savor that one!

Fortunately, most married women will remain your friends. They can live vicariously through your new adventures . . . suffering your tragedies and, most importantly, learning from your mistakes. They'll also be looking for ways to judge their own relationships. And don't forget: they, too, have fertile fantasies, and can be a valuable source of information. The relationship will blossom as you get to act out their wildest dreams!

49. **An ex-husband can be used as a great topic of conversation.** Especially when you and your friends get together. "Creative tension release" is an acceptable term for these truly therapeutic "bull sessions." Notice how much easier it is to giggle when someone else's "Ex" acts crazy? Even when it's the same damn thing *your* "Ex" is doing?!

50. **An ex-husband can be used to motivate you and your friends.** You can all unite to rid yourselves of all those ex-husband once and for all. Just start a chain letter to all divorced women. Ask each to wrap and send her ex-husband to the woman whose name appears at the top of the list. It will add spice — and a variety of men — to your life, and ensure that some other poor woman ends up with your "Ex."

Imagine the fun you and your friends will have deciding who to send *your* ex-husband to!

CHAPTER 7

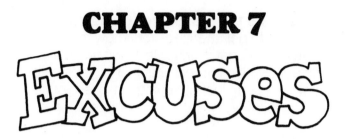

One of the best things about an ex-husband is that you can use him as an excuse. Unless you've been asleep in the deep woods, you already know that.

An ex-husband can be used as an excuse for avoiding anything you don't like or don't want to do. How is he going to defend himself? Who wouldn't believe a sweetheart like you?

Since the first day you met him — and definitely since the last days of the divorce — you've used him for all kinds of excuses: "Sorry, I can't make the party. Ratfink has to work late tonight." And: "I'd love to come over and hear how you passed that kidney stone, Dad, but Ratfink has the flu and can't be left alone."

Ratfink's been your excuse for years. You've blamed him or his family for virtually anything and everything. Now start using it to your advantage! Learn to take charge of your life again!

You're probably pretty creative at this already. But just in case you have been asleep in the woods, or suffer from chronic mental block, here are a few thought-provokers.

51. **Use your ex-husband as the reason your kids make bad grades in school.** Kids sometimes "play dumb" to get attention. You know they're not *really* stupid, but teachers don't. Tell their teachers that they unfortunately inherited their father's lack of motivation. After all, you were a straight "A" student with a promising career in nuclear physics until you married him. Don't forget to stress the hours you spend working with them, proving that even your quality environment can't overcome such a severe genetic deficiency as Ratfink's laziness. Of course, if the kids improve their grades, you take full credit.

52. **Use your ex-husband as an excuse when your kids skip classes at school.** It's certainly not *your* fault! They must have learned it from their father. Heaven knows he skipped home often enough! Explain to their principal that you're working hard to overcome their father's negative influence. Then give the principal Ratfink's number. If nothing else, it'll take the heat off you.

53. **Use your ex-husband to explain why your kids go through fads.** Especially something like "punk" clothing and green, Mohawk hairstyles. Just tell anyone who asks, and even those who don't, that they look just like their father.

54. **Use your ex-husband as an excuse for staying in group therapy.** The group is great for moral support, plenty of hugs, and lots of attention. They allow you to be you. It's a safe place to practice assertiveness and there's no fear of rejection. It's the next best thing to a mother's womb. Besides, you haven't gone out with the therapist yet. You'd like to find out if he really practices what he preaches.

55. **Use your ex-husband as an excuse for redecorating the house.** After all, you don't want it to look the way it did when Ratfink lived there. That would only bring back painful memories. So you have a choice. Spend the money on redecorating, or spend it on more sessions with your shrink. Your friends will think you made a wise decision. Of course, your shrink won't.

56. **Use your ex-husband as an excuse for going bonkers on a new wardrobe.** Throw in a new hairstyle and some acrylic nails, too. People expect this from a divorced woman. Don't disappoint your public! Now that Ratfink's gone, you want your "outside" to reflect the way you feel on the "inside" — GREAT!!

57. **Use your ex-husband as an excuse for your dog's un-neighborly behavior.** When your neighbors complain about the brown spots in their yards, blame Ratfink. After all, it's *his* dog. He wanted it. He trained it. Then he left it with you. And it's hard to teach an old dog new tricks. Besides, if they think the dog's social graces are bad, they should see Ratfink's!

58. **Use your ex-husband as an excuse for your bad moods.** When someone notices that you're a bit on edge, even downright nasty, blame it on your "Ex." Tell them that you started out the day "in such a good mood, then Ratfink called!" Blaming him gives you some variety for explaining bad moods. Before, you were stuck with boring excuses about hormones and Pre-Menstrual Syndrome.

59. **Use your ex-husband as an excuse to cover your late arrivals.** When you show up an hour late for work…when you arrive during dessert at a dinner party…when you just catch the last hymn at church. Hold your head up high. With Ratfink, you'll always have the perfect excuse.

60. **Use your ex-husband as an excuse for avoiding dull social events.** If he wasn't invited, say you have to bail him out of jail…again. If he was invited, just say you don't feel emotionally able to deal with him yet. Actually, you're afraid you might die laughing if you have to watch that socially inept slob make a fool of himself in public.

61. **Use your ex-husband as an excuse for not inviting Joe Blow in for a nightcap.** Sometimes you end up with a date that no one deserves. In one way or another, this guy actually makes Ratfink look good!! But you're just too nice to hurt his feelings. Ratfink to the rescue! Simply tell Mr. Blow that your "Ex" is baby-sitting…that he hasn't adjusted well to the divorce…that he carries a loaded shotgun. Problem solved.

62. **Use your ex-husband as an excuse when you over-indulge.** With an ex-husband, you have a perfectly valid excuse for occasionally drowning your sorrows. Like the day you drank a bottle of Jim Beam, smoked a carton of Kools, and devoured an entire case of Mrs. Smith's Pies. Ratfink's unique. He drives you *beyond* mere drink.

63. **Use your ex-husband as an excuse for late and unpaid bills.** Quiver your lower lip, hang your head to one side, and let a few small tears roll down your cheeks while you humbly explain that your alimony check is late again. It won't make a bit of difference to the bill collector, but it sure beats the heck out of saying "the check's in the mail."

Whatever happens, use Ratfink as your excuse. Let's face it: there were many times over the years when he blamed you for his foul-ups and blunders. And there were just as many times when he failed to give you the credit you deserved for his successes. The time has finally come to reverse that trend. Start taking the credit you're due!

CHAPTER 8

An ex-husband can be used to make your life run more smoothly when it comes to dealing with the kids. First, let's face facts: a tomcat is more interested in and involved with his kids than Rat-fink was during your marriage. But the divorce has changed that. Typically, an ex-husband spends more time with his kids after the divorce than before. Some of this is due to the children's innate ability to manipulate a situation to their own advantage. Those "angels" know just how to use their father's guilt to get what they want, whether it's a raise in their allowance or a new ten-speed bike. And because he's trying hard to look like the good guy, he's much more agreeable to their demands. Use that to *your* advantage, too!

64. **Use your ex-husband to explain the "birds and the bees" to the children.** This will save you a lot of aggravation. Perhaps even a good deal of embarrassment. Besides, your parents never explained it to you. They just gave you some dumb book to read.

So even though you were the one to explain the birds and the bees to Ratfink on your honeymoon, the job is better left to him. After all, he's on this "togetherness" kick, so the chance to spend some "quality time" with the kids is to his advantage. The kids have probably heard it all before, but they'll love watching him squirm.

65. **Use your ex-husband to discipline the kids.** One of your biggest problems these days is that the kids are beginning to think their father is the ninth wonder of the world. This is called the "Disney Daddy Syndrome." When he's with the kids, they have nothing but fun. No chores and no discipline — unless you count "eat all of your banana split" as discipline!

With Daddy, it's tours of the Grand Canyon…sailing at the Cape…visits to Disney World. The kids think wonderful thoughts about Daddy the Tour Guide, and lousy thoughts about Mommy the Ogre.

With a little reverse psychology, you can change all that. When the kids don't cooperate, scream: "Well, you'll just have to go camping with your father!!" Until that moment, the kids were looking forward to it. Now they're not so sure. Of course, sooner or later they'll catch on, but until then, you can keep your sanity: "That's it! I've had enough! I'm going to have your father take you to Disney World if you don't behave!"

66. **Use your ex-husband to take the children on those special father-kid outings.** The ones you'd rather not attend. Volunteer Ratfink when there's a chance of unwanted bug bites, sunburn, and a peeling nose. Send him to school field days, where he can stand out in the hot sun watching little kids fall flat on their faces in sack races. Let him chaperone field trips to the zoo. He and the monkeys will get along great. Camping trips are also good. You have no desire to become a junior cub scout…to learn how to cook over an open fire, pitch a tent, or bait a hook.

Of course, there *are* exceptions. Some of those scout leaders have great looking legs. Play your cards right and you'll have them cooking your meals, pitching your tent, and baiting your hook. The same holds true for school outings. If there are enough fathers chaperoning, it might prove interesting. Think about it.

67. **Use your ex-husband as a summer camp.** Summer is no vacation with the kids telling you "there's nothing to do" five hundred times a day. But there's no way you're going to shell out big bucks to send them to Camp Snoopy so they can learn how to short-sheet beds. Peace and quiet can be achieved another way.

Send them to Ratfink for the summer. Don't you want to find out how many trips to Sea World he can make before he has to deal with their boredom? How long before he hears "Mom doesn't make us do it that way!"? Heaven knows you've heard it about him all year along! Summer means it's his turn.

68. **Use your ex-husband to take the kids "trick or treating."** Let's face it. Halloween can be fun for both adults and children. But not necessarily if they are together.

Let your "Ex" deal with the costume traumas. Have him explain to the kids why they can't go as a Chinese Dragon or an 8-foot high man. Let him handle the broken zippers, lost masks and dead flashlight batteries. He can suffer through the temper tantrums when it's time to stop for the night and they've only covered half the county. He can settle the arguments over who has the most candy, and mastermind the trading. You never did think a candy apple was worth two chocolate bars anyway.

In return for allowing him this "quality time" with the kids, you can go to a masquerade ball…hopefully with your new boyfriend.

69. **Use your ex-husband to fill-in for you at parent-teacher conferences.** Don't you have a tennis lesson? Or a final exam in glass blowing? Why in the world would you want to sit there while the teacher tells you how far the kid's grades have slipped? Let Ratfink take the heat. It's his fault anyway. After all, if he wasn't trying to be a "Disney Daddy," and had enforced some discipline like you begged, none of this would be necessary!

He'll probably go to the conference gladly, to put the make on the teacher. Too bad the teacher's a man. Too bad you've already dated him.

70.

Use your ex-husband for all the Christmas Eve dirty work. Why should you be stuck trying to assemble a bike? And what do you have in common with the King Kong Erector Set? Doll carriages may be fun, but not when the directions call for four wheels and you only have three. Let Ratfink put the toys together.

Christmas Eve is meant for snuggly fires, warm eggnog, soft music and a reasonably sexy companion. Even if those are not available, it's still not meant for hard labor. Use Ratfink. Invite him over to share Christmas Eve with the kiddies. Won't he be surprised!

71.

Use your ex-husband to stay up with the kids on New Year's Eve. And be certain that he's the one to get up with them the next morning. Of course, this will take some doing. But remember, you've had the kids for most of Christmas vacation. It's only fair they get some time to be with Daddy, too. He might be suspicious. Especially after you tricked him on Christmas Eve. So just point out that you know how much he loves his New Year's Day football. Offer to pick the kids up by noon so he can stay glued to the tube without interruption. Throw in a pizza or two. It will work. At least once. Just try not to feel too guilty New Year's Eve, knowing that he's stuck with the kids while you're stuck at that wonderful party!

CHAPTER 9

Convenience

An ex-husband is truly a convenient thing to have. Even if he is insensitive, immoral, selfish, and just plain wacky. At least now you know how to use him as motivation for keeping you healthy. You can use what you've learned from dealing with him to grasp the fine points of financial management, and to explore new career opportunities. Not only can he be useful in establishing an exciting sex life, but he can also help you improve your relationships with family and friends. You can use him to eliminate hassles with the kids, to get things done around the house, and to serve as an excuse for copping-out on anything you want.

And, as if that wasn't enough, there are dozens of miscellaneous ways you can use him as a convenience in your new life.

72. **Use your ex-husband to train your new Doberman guard-dog.** No, don't have Ratfink train the dog for you. Train the dog on him. See the difference? Instead of trying to train Ratfink to call before he comes by, train the dog to attack on sight.

Start out by housebreaking the puppy. Use Ratfink's old clothes instead of newspapers. Eventually the dog will get the scent and the idea. This will provide marvelous entertainment whenever Ratfink's around. And if he overstays his welcome, just call the dog to do his thing.

73. **Use your ex-husband's address and telephone number when you don't want to use your own.** Like the other day when you were shopping and that skinny, four-eyed jerk kept trying to hustle you. Or last night at the local hot-spot, when that dumb gorilla wouldn't leave you alone. Don't break out in a cold sweat, fearful that someone you know might notice. Just say "OK, big boy, I'd *love* for you to give me a call." Then give him a fake name and Ratfink's phone number.

74. **Use your ex-husband to improve your underwear collection.** The dowdy flannel nightgowns Ratfink gave you no longer fit with your exciting lifestyle. Besides, they just prove that he wanted a mother-figure and not the sex-goddess you've always been. It's time you go on a shopping spree. Another one. Visit Frederick's of Hollywood for black negligees, French bras, silk stockings, and crotchless panties. And remember to send Ratfink the bill.

75. **Use your ex-husband to try out new recipes before serving them to your boyfriend.** Ratfink is always ready to bum a free meal. Treat him to "something special." With your new zest for life, you've started to experiment with some really far-out concoctions. Like "Squid a l'Orange." It sounds awful, but who really knows? Give it a shot. Just make sure the first shot isn't with your latest beau. The dog, the cat, and the kids have all been running for cover whenever you announce "something special" for dinner. Why alienate them any further?

76. **Use your ex-husband as a food tester.** Have you ever noticed how food that looks yummy one day can grow some pretty strange stuff on it the next? Sometimes that's normal for the food, and sometimes it's not. Don't take a chance on botulism for yourself, the kids, or the pets. Use Ratfink to test for food poisoning. You've seen some of his dates. He has a pretty strong stomach.

Just because something's been left in the refrigerator for a month or so doesn't mean it's spoiled. This is nothing to be ashamed of either. It happens to the best people. Hey, it's not unusual to find some Thanksgiving leftovers the day before Christmas. Sometimes it happens in the *same* year! And with rising prices, you have to watch the food budget. Ratfink's been hinting that you owe him a meal. Serve him your findings. You can kill two birds with one stone…not literally, of course.

77. **Use your ex-husband as a late-night "Hotline."** This is especially handy if you were up late because the kids were sick or had a big school project due the next day. It's only fair that you share these woes with Ratfink. Remember, there was a time when he loved to talk to you on the phone for hours on end, no matter how late it was. And besides, your friends have started getting a little ticked off about your 2:00 a.m. calls.

78. **Use your ex-husband as a cure for insomnia.** Just call Ratfink and it won't be long before you're fast asleep. Remember how boring he was at 3:00 a.m. — even in the best of times? Come to think of it, he was pretty boring at 1:00 a.m. *And* 1:00 p.m.

This might sound like a contradiction. On one hand, he's a late-night hotline. On the other, he's a cure for insomnia. But there *is* a difference. As a hotline, you do all the talking which calms you down so you can sleep. As a cure for insomnia, let him do the talking. His monotone will have you comatose in no time.

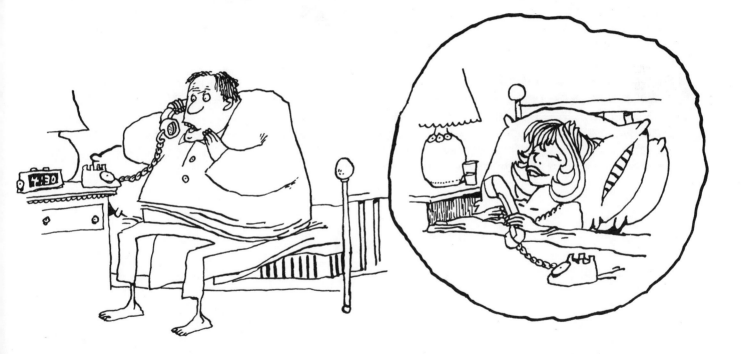

79. **Use your ex-husband to test the water for sharks.** You never know what's lurking beneath the surface. Many people who saw "Jaws" wished they had an ex-husband. Many were afraid to go in the water. Some were afraid to go in their pools! See how lucky you are? Have him test for jellyfish, temperature, and undertows, too.

By the way, over the last few years there's been an increase in shark attacks. On men…formerly married men. *You* figure it out.

80. **Use your ex-husband as a house-sitter.** You know how hard it is to find someone to take care of the pets, the plants, and the newspapers while you're away. Why not use Ratfink? Besides, he'd love the opportunity to snoop around the house.

Of course, you'll have to write down every little detail. Describe which plants need water and how often. Elaborate on how much to feed the pets and when. And don't forget the fish. Tell him they need to be "finger-fed." Just don't tell him they're man-eating piranhas.

81. Use your ex-husband as a navigator and source for directions.

For years he told you where to go anyway. Be honest. Doesn't he win the award for the *Most Nervous Passenger* you ever had in your car? And wasn't he always navigating?

So give him the job. Next time you're lost late at night, call him: "Well, Rat honey, I'm here at the Dynamite Disco and I want to get to the Adonis Bar & Grill. What's the best way at this hour?"

Who knows the way to the airport, the cruise ship terminal, or Plato's Retreat better? When you're sitting around late at night, planning flights of fantasy, call him to make sure there won't be any navigational problems. He's been sleeping too much lately anyhow.

82. Use your ex-husband as a ladder tester.

Sometimes cats do the darndest things. They climb up into high places then act like they can't get down. You know they will, but try telling that to the kids. It's been quite a while since you've had the old ladder out of the garage. Even longer since you climbed it! And you'll be damned if you're going to climb a ladder you're not sure of to rescue a cat that can return to earth on its own. But try telling *that* to the kids!

It's time to call Ratfink. He'll love the opportunity to impress the kids (and you) with his bravado. The odds are good that he'll go up the ladder. But, if he loses his nerve (or locates his senses) let him be the one to call the fire department.

83. **Use your ex-husband as the fourth in card games.** Bridge comes to mind. You need a dummy hand — who would be a better choice? Try to avoid calling him if the game is strip poker. After all, pointing and laughing at someone's body is really cruel.

84. **Use your ex-husband's departure to do what *you* want after the kids are asleep.** Remember the good old days? Just when you thought you could sit down and watch your favorite show, he'd turn on some stupid shoot-em-up. Same plot every week. Ten minutes of dialogue, and the rest of the show was car chases and busting into bordellos. He even wanted to watch the re-runs!

Now you can watch anything you want. You can go to fast food restaurants when you don't feel like cooking. You don't even have to worry about lounging around in your underwear. It wasn't that you were shy. It was that he thought you were feeling sexy, and felt obligated to satisfy you — usually by offering his back for you to scratch. Sometimes he'd get really wild and crazy, and ask for a foot massage. Ratfink really knew how to satisfy a woman!

85. **Use your ex-husband's departure to make yourself at home.** You haven't lost a husband. You've gained a closet, a bathroom, a workroom, and a garage. To have and to hold, and all that.

Why did he have to have all that closet space? "Because I have to look my best for work — I bring home the bacon!" What a weak argument for having you spread your clothes in half a dozen closets throughout the house. Besides, he even forgot to bring himself home towards the end!

And what about the bathroom? Toss all that macho aftershave and manly dedorant in the trash. No more beard stubble clogging the sink. No more of his towels on the floor. You can hang your pantyhose any damn place you please! And you won't have to listen to him scream bloody murder after you've used his razor on your legs. The only problem will be remembering to buy your own razor blades. Consider it a fair trade-off.

86. Use your ex-husband to balance your checkbook. Why be bothered by such trivia as "will this check bounce?" Let Ratfink worry about all that.

Just don't show him the checks. After all, you don't want him to know where you're spending your money. Let him do the balancing blind. Or write all your checks to "cash."

If he gets annoyed with that, use the "double-entry system." Make the checks out to the right party, but log them in the book under names he'll find acceptable. When he sees how low your balance is, and how much you spend on the kids, he might even add some extra money to his child support payments.

Alright. So that's *not* very likely. It's *still* a good idea to pawn mundane garbage like balancing checkbooks off on him!

87. Use your ex-husband as a butler or bartender for your parties. There are several things to consider before doing this. First, does Ratfink have problems thinking and breathing at the same time? Try to be objective. It's possible his familiarity with the house will help compensate for his ineptitude.

Second, have you told your escort what a monster Ratfink is? If so, you wouldn't want him to find out that you exaggerated a bit.

Otherwise, this gives you a golden opportunity to look stunning, and to show Ratfink that you have a whole new circle of friends who find you intelligent, interesting, attractive, and witty.

88. **Use your ex-husband as a cheap date.** Let's say you're really bored, and all the friends, acquaintances, and total strangers you've called are busy. Call Ratfink. Tell him there are some important matters you need to discuss concerning the kids, finances, the car, or whatever. The "why" is not important. Just tell him you'll buy dinner. He'll accept. He certainly won't pass up the opportunity to see you if he thinks you're down.

Handle it right, and the odds are good that he'll pay for dinner. If not, at least you'll get out of the house. You'll also get to practice your fantasies, by pretending he's James Bond and not Ratfink. Otherwise, you'll never make it through dinner.

89. **Use your ex-husband to test new hair colorings.** Offer to give him a shampoo, a scalp rub, and a free snack. Then point out his grey hairs and offer to help. If he's going to date nineteen-year-old cheerleaders, he's going to have to keep the hair looking good.

Once you've got him, find out whether the hair coloring you were planning to use really *does* match your own color. You might even discover you have a talent for mixing and matching. He might even discover that he looks good as a redhead.

90. **Use your ex-husband to perfect your haircutting techniques.** Don't tell him it's practice. Just casually mention that you have been studying "coiffure design" at the local Academe du Hair. Lie a little and tell him you got a degree. Throw in something about making it a career. Whatever you do, don't practice on the kids. If you make a mistake with them, you'll have to live with their complaints for months.

91. Use your ex-husband as a safe escort.

There are many times when you get invited to a fancy social outing...the kind where it's inappropriate to arrive unescorted. This can cause problems. Your first choice might be busy. Or you may not want to choose one and offend the others. Then again, you might not want to take any of the men you've been seeing. They're alright for private occasions, but they're all wrong for public display.

Don't cheat yourself out of a good time. Call Ratfink. True, he is a boring escort. But at least he's safe. None of your boyfriends will be offended that you went with him. And so what if they get worried that you're trying to reconcile. They'll only become more attentive. As for any concern about sexual advances, fear not. That's an area *you* control now.

Just try not to treat Ratfink as poorly at your social function as he used to treat you at his. No leaving him the minute you walk into the room. No wandering off for hours to talk sports, sex, or shop with a group of your cronies. And for crying out loud, don't go drinking too much and coming on to anything and everything in pants! You'd *hate* to embarrass him to tears...wouldn't you?

92. **Use your ex-husband to relieve your frustrations.** Kids got you down? Troubles at work? Take it out on Ratfink. Call his secretary and leave the number for "Dial-A-Prayer," "Susie Wong's Massage Parlor," or "Dr. Peter's Sex Shoppe." Put him on the Prison Pen-Pal mailing list. Fill out subscription cards in his name for magazines you know he'll despise.

When you get *really* angry at something he's done, give his name to a cemetery plot salesman. Volunteer him for medical research. Call his new girlfriend and pretend you're a newer girlfriend. Have all your friends call the Herpes Emergency Hotline and report Ratfink by name. He'll really love you for it.

93. **Use your ex-husband as a source for jokes.** Over the years, there have been many trends in jokes. There have been Traveling Salesman Jokes, Moron Jokes, and Truly Tasteless Jokes. Use your experiences to set a new trend with Ratfink Jokes! Remember: some magazines pay good money for good jokes. And heaven knows, Ratfink was enough of a Truly Tasteless Traveling Moron to provide years of entertainment.

94. **Use your ex-husband when you want to regress to childhood — or at least feel younger.** Remember some of those nasty childhood pranks? Wouldn't it be fun to relive them? Soap Ratfink's windows. Toilet paper his yard. Dump garbage on his front step. Ring his door bell and run like hell! He'd never have you arrested. If he did, the kids would be living with him.

95.

Use your ex-husband to establish neighborhood harmony. Before the divorce, the next-door neighbors couldn't decide whether you were a witch or he was a worm. Now that the divorce is over, the truth can be told: he was a worm.

Take your neighbors some chocolate chip cookies. Thank them for not taking sides during the divorce. Careful though — your neighbor's husband thinks you are now fair game. He knows how long it's been since the separation and figures you're horny as hell. He'll let you know that if he can be of *any* service, *any* time, you just have to call.

Have you ever seen a grown man drool like that? And that wink of his could make a sailor seasick. Just hope he doesn't talk in his sleep, or your neighbor might be asking your advice on handling *her* "Ex"!

96.

Use your ex-husband to make your dates more thrilling. Frequently after a divorce, the man decides he has wasted his life and tries to make up for lost time. He takes on new challenges, trying desperately to impress those sweet, young things he's dating. Maybe he's trying to prove he hasn't lost his courage.

Who cares why he's doing it? Watching Ratfink face Death can be an extremely entertaining date for you and your new boyfriend. Just make doubly sure he's insured. To the hilt! And that you and the kids are the beneficiaries. Once that's all been confirmed, encourage him.

97. **Use your ex-husband to wait at your place for repairmen.** You know the scenario. They say they'll be there first thing Tuesday morning. When you get them on the phone, they say they meant *next* Tuesday. Why not use Ratfink to wait in your place? It will give him another chance to snoop, while you get a day at the beach with your boyfriend!

98. **Use your ex-husband to argue with service people.** Is the garage attendant trying to overcharge you? Call Ratfink to the rescue! After all, what do you know about mechanical thingamabobs? Look sad and dejected when you ask Ratfink for help. Boost his ego. Tell him how well he always handles these things. Promise to handle it better next time. And when it comes time to pay, tell him you forgot your wallet. Promise to pay him back. Don't.

99.

Use your ex-husband to take the kids to the doctor (or the dentist or the orthodontist). There are a few things worse than sitting in a crowded waiting room, reading a two-year old magazine, with a kid who can't stand to be there. One of those few things is when it's finally your turn to go in.

Do you really want to listen to a lecture about feeding the kid more of the foods he hates? Do you really want to sit and listen to the dentist's screams after the kid bites his hand…again? Do you really want to explain why, for the tenth time, the bands are off, the wires are broken, and the retainer is never worn? Hardly! Let Ratfink take the heat!

115

100. **Use your ex-husband to take the kids shopping for back-to-school clothes and supplies.** What truly signals the end of summer? Not the swallows leaving Capistrano. Not even your fading suntan. It's the newspaper ads for Back-to-School Sales!

Here's how to avoid this nightmare. Time one of Ratfink's weekends just before the beginning of school. Have the kids circle items in ads and catalogs for all the things they need (and want). Get them good and pumped.

When Ratfink comes to pick them up, remind him that it's no big deal. Just a short shopping trip, lasting maybe an hour. Try not to laugh. Point out that the kids are excited about school and thrilled that their Dad is getting involved. Explain that they each have a list (remember all those circled ads?), and tell him he can make the trip go faster by taking all the kids at one time. He'll believe it…once!

101. Above all, use your ex-husband to choose mates more wisely in the future.

A typical first reaction to divorce is "Never Again!!" Your first urge is to move to an island somewhere where there are no men. There are all kinds of promises to avoid involvement and live the life of a nun. Statistical evidence shows, however, that these first reactions are rarely followed.

Many people go from divorce to a new marriage with the same kind of person. Too often, they end up repeating the same kind of mistakes.

If you want different results, you have to take different steps. Perhaps you were too much the "giver" in the first relationship. If so, you should try to be more of a "requirer" next time around. It's not easy to change, so take it a step at a time.

If you've paid attention to this book, you will have come to the realization that an ex-husband *can* be useful in many areas of your life. That's important, because to improve the odds on your next relationship, you need to put the last one in perspective. Instead of looking only at the disadvantages, take note of the advantages. If nothing else, it's a much better view.

So you see, an ex-husband truly is a good thing to have. Hold your head high. Put a sparkle in your eye. You *don't* need a man to make you feel like somebody. And you certainly don't need Ratfink!! His cooperation can sometimes help make your life a little easier, but you *can* live without him.

Read and re-read **101 Uses.** Put it to work for you. And make up your mind, here and now, that you're going to teach that ex-husband of yours to treat you right.

Even if it kills him.

101 USES FOR AN EX-HUSBAND

If you liked the book, you'll love these gifts!

☐ **Coffee Mugs** ☐ **T-Shirts**
☐ **1986 Calendar** ☐ **Poster**
☐ **Bumper Stickers** ☐ **Buttons**

And another delightful book from John C. Yurick:

"If It Weren't For Stupid People..."

A book dealing with the problems of daily living, from relationships, sex, and jealousy to neighbors, kids, and jobs. 104 pages. Send $4.95 plus sales tax and $1.50 postage and handling.

☐ Please send me more information about the items checked.

☐ Please send me_____ **"If It Weren't For Stupid People..."**

My ☐ Check ☐ Money Order for $_____is enclosed.

NAME _____

ADDRESS_____

CITY_____STATE _____ ZIP_____

Send coupon to: **"101 Uses"**
                          P.O. Box 1956
                          Maitland, FL 32751

And if you liked the book, order another!

For additional copies of this delightful book, visit your local bookstore, or send $6.95 plus sales tax and $1.50 postage and handling.

☐ Please send me___copies of **"101 Uses For An Ex-Husband"**
☐ Check ☐ Visa ☐ Mastercard   Expiration Date_____
Acct. No._____
Signature_____

NAME _____

ADDRESS_____

CITY_____STATE _____ ZIP_____

Send coupon to: **Currier•Davis Publishing**
                      P.O. Box 58
                      Winter Park, FL 32790-0058